Walt Whitman

Quotes... Vol.20

by The Secret Libraries

Kindle EDITION

The Secret Libraries

Published by The Secret Libraries
www.thesecretlibraries.com
Annotation and Artists Background by The Secret Libraries 2016

Paperback:
ISBN-13: 978-1540743459
ISBN-10: 1540743454

Quotes...

This book provides a selected collection of 200 quotes from the works of Walt Whitman.

Walt Whitman

1819-1892

Resist much, obey little.

"

Be curious, not judgmental.

"

It is a beautiful truth that all men contain something of the artist in them. And perhaps it is the case that the greatest artists live and die, the world and themselves alike ignorant what they possess.

Keep your face always toward the sunshine - and shadows will fall behind you.

"

We were together. I forget the rest.

"

Some people are so much sunlight to the square inch. I am still bathing in the cheer he radiated.

Nothing can happen more beautiful than death.

Each of us inevitable; Each of us limitless—each of us with his or her right upon the earth.

"

I have no mockings or arguments; I witness and wait.

"

14

Over all the sky—the sky! far, far out of reach, studded with the eternal stars.

In the faces of men and women I see God.

The great city is that which has the greatest man or woman.

Give me the splendid silent sun, with all his beams full-dazzling.

Lo, the moon ascending! Up from the East, the silvery round moon; Beautiful over the house-tops, ghastly, phantom moon; Immense and silent moon.

Beautiful that war and all its deeds of carnage, must

in time be utterly lost; That the hands of the sisters Death and Night incessantly softly wash again and ever again, this soiled world.

I will write the evangel-poem of comrades and of love.

In this broad earth of ours, Amid the measureless grossness and the slag, Enclosed and safe within its central heart, Nestles the seed perfection.

If the United States haven't grown poets, on any scale of grandeur, it is certain that they import, print, and read more poetry than any equal number of people elsewhere -- probably more than the rest of the world combined. Poetry (like a grand personality) is a growth of many generations -- many rare combinations. To have great poets, there must be great audiences too.

When lilacs last in the door-yard bloomed, And the great star early drooped in the western sky in the night, I mourned, and yet shall mourn with ever-returning spring.

All, all for immortality, Love like the light silently wrapping all.

"

Liberty is to be subserved, whatever occurs.

"

Come lovely and soothing death, Undulate round the world, serenely arriving, arriving, In the day, in the night, to all, to each, Sooner or later, delicate death.

We Americans have yet to really learn our own antecedents, and sort them, to unify them. They will be found ampler than has been supposed, and in widely different sources. Thus far, impress'd by New England writers and schoolmasters, we tacitly abandon ourselves to the notion that our United States has been fashion'd from the British Islands only, and essentially form a second England only — which is a very great mistake.

I say the real and permanent grandeur of these States must be their religion.

Thunder on! Stride on! Democracy. Strike with vengeful stroke!

I say the whole earth and all the stars in the sky are for religion's sake.

Youth, large, lusty, loving—Youth, full of grace, force, fascination!
Do you know that Old Age may come after you, with equal grace, force, fascination?

Roaming in thought over the Universe, I saw the little that is Good steadily hastening towards immortality, and the vast that is evil I saw hastening to merge itself and become lost and dead.

None has begun to think how divine he himself is and how certain the future is.

What is that you express in your eyes? It seems to me more than all the print I have read in my life.

Do I contradict myself? Very well, then, I contradict myself; I am large -- I contain multitudes.

Not I, nor anyone else can travel that road for you. You must travel it by yourself. It is not far. It is within reach. Perhaps you have been on it since you were born, and did not know. Perhaps it is everywhere - on water and land.

Whatever satisfies the soul is truth.

"

I am large, I contain multitudes.

"

"

I have learned that to be with those I like is enough.

"

"

I loafe and invite my soul.

"

I sound my barbaric yawp over the roofs of the world.

I have just this moment heard from the front — there is nothing yet of a movement, but each side is continually on the alert, expecting something to happen.

O Banner!

Not houses of peace are you, nor any nor all of their prosperity; if need be you shall have every one of those houses to destroy them; You thought not to destroy those valuable houses, standing fast, full of comfort, built with money; May they stand fast then? Not an hour, unless you, above them and all, stand fast.

Happiness, not in another place but this place...not for another hour, but this hour.

Do anything, but let it produce joy.

I am as bad as the worst, but, thank God, I am as good as the best.

Failing to fetch me at first, keep encouraged. Missing me one place, search another. I stop somewhere waiting for you.

I like the scientific spirit—the holding off, the being sure but not too sure, the willingness to surrender ideas when the evidence is against them: this is ultimately fine—it always keeps the way beyond open—always gives life, thought, affection, the whole man, a chance to try over again after a mistake—after a wrong guess.

I exist as I am, that is enough, If no other in the world be aware I sit content, And if each and all be aware I sit content. One world is aware, and by the far the largest to me, and that is myself, And whether I come to my own today or in ten thousand or ten million years, I can cheerfully take it now, or with equal cheerfulness, I can wait.

"

Peace is always beautiful.

„

I discover myself on the verge of a usual mistake.

Pointing to another world will never stop vice among us; shedding light over this world can alone help us.

God is a mean-spirited, pugnacious bully bent on revenge against his children for failing to live up to his impossible standards.

These are the days that must happen to you.

I do not ask the wounded person how he feels, I myself become the wounded person.

The art of art, the glory of expression and the sunshine of the light of letters, is simplicity.

Whoever you are, now I place my hand upon you/ That you may be my poem/ I whisper with my lips close to your ear/ I have loved many women and men, but I love none better than you.

Note, to-day, an instructive, curious spectacle and conflict.

Science, (twin, in its fields, of Democracy in its)—Science, testing absolutely all thoughts, all works, has already burst well upon the world—a sun, mounting, most illuminating, most glorious—surely never again to set. But against it, deeply entrench'd, holding possession, yet remains, (not only through the churches and schools, but by imaginative literature, and unregenerate poetry,) the fossil theology of the mythic-materialistic, superstitious, untaught and credulous, fable-loving, primitive ages of humanity.

Afoot and lighthearted I take to the open road, healthy, free, the world before me.

If you done it, it ain't bragging.

Battles are lost in the same spirit in which they are won.

If you want me again look for me under your boot soles.

" "

And as to me, I know nothing else but miracles.

" "

Re-examine all you have been told. Dismiss what insults your soul.

"

I am satisfied ... I see, dance, laugh, sing.

"

I believe a leaf of grass is no less than the journey-work of the stars.

Now I see the secret of making the best person: it is to grow in the open air and to eat and sleep with the earth.

I too am not a bit tamed, I too am untranslatable.

I exist as I am, that is enough.

I celebrate myself, and sing myself, And what I assume you shall assume, For every atom belonging to me as good belongs to you.

The real war will never get in the books.

Every moment of light and dark is a miracle.

Give me the splendid, silent sun with all his beams full-dazzling.

Argue not concerning God,...re-examine all that you have been told at church or school or in any book, dismiss whatever insults your soul...

All goes onward and outward, nothing collapses,
And to die is different from what any one supposed, and luckier.

"

I tramp a perpetual journey.

I cannot be awake, for nothing looks to me as it did before, or else I am awake for the first time, and all before has been a mean sleep.

A morning-glory at my window satisfies me more than the metaphysics of books.

From this hour I ordain myself loos'd of limits and imaginary lines.

All beauty comes from beautiful blood and a beautiful brain. If the greatnesses are in conjunction in a man or woman it is enough...the fact will prevail through the universe...but the gaggery and gilt of a million years will not prevail. Who troubles himself about his ornaments or fluency is lost. This is what you shall so: Love the earth and sun and the animals, despise riches, give alms to every one that asks, stand up for the stupid and crazy, devote your income and labor to others, hate tyrants, argue not concerning God, have patience and indulgence toward the people, take off your hat to nothing known or unknown or to any man or number of men, go freely with powerful uneducated persons and with the young and with the mothers of families, read these leaves in the open air every season of every year of your life, re-examine all you have been told at school or church or in any book, dismiss whatever insults your own soul, and your very flesh shall be a great poem and have the richest fluency not only in its words but in the silent lines of its lips and face and between the lashes of your eyes and in every motion and joint of your body...

"

There is no God any more divine than Yourself.

"

"

The future is no more uncertain than the present.

"

Love the earth and sun and animals.

Stranger, if you passing meet me and desire to speak to me, why should you not speak to me? And why should I not speak to you?

I act as the tongue of you...tied in your mouth...in mine it begins to be loosened.

I hear and behold God in every object, yet understand God not in the least.

Afoot and light-hearted I take to the open road. Healthy, free, the world before me. The long brown path before me leading me wherever I choose. Henceforth, I ask not good fortune, I myself am good fortune. Henceforth, I whimper no more, postpone no more, need nothing.

A writer can do nothing for men more necessary, satisfying, than just simply to reveal to them the infinite possibility of their own souls.

Now, Voyager, sail thou forth, to seek and find.

"

You will hardly know who I am or what I mean.

"

My words itch at your ears till you understand them.

Touch me, touch the palm of your hand to my body as I pass, Be not afraid of my body.

To me, every hour of the day and night is an unspeakably perfect miracle.

I Think it is lost.....but nothing is ever lost nor can be lost. The body sluggish, aged, cold, the ember left from earlier fires shall duly flame again.

I will sleep no more but arise, You oceans that have been calm within me! how I feel you, fathomless, stirring, preparing unprecedented waves and storms.

This hour I tell things in confidence/ I might not tell everybody, but I will tell you.

"

It makes such difference where you read.

"

I will You, in all, Myself, with promise to never desert you,
To which I sign my name.

But where is what I started for so long ago? And why is it yet unfound?

If anything is sacred, the human body is sacred.

I swear to you, there are divine things more beautiful than words can tell.

You shall no longer take things at second or third hand, not look through the eyes of the dead, nor feed on the spectres in books. You shall not look through my eyes either, nor take things from me, you shall listen to all sides and filter them from yourself.

Loafe with me on the grass—loose the stop from your throat; Not words, not music or rhyme I want—not custom or lecture, not even the best; Only the lull I like, the hum of your valved voice.

The road to wisdom is paved with excess. The mark of a true writer is their ability to mystify the familiar and familiarize the strange.

The powerful play goes on and you may contribute a verse.

The secret of it all, is to write in the gush, the throb, the

flood, of the moment – to put things down without deliberation –
without worrying about their style – without waiting for a fit time or
place. I always worked that way. I took the first scrap of paper, the
first doorstep, the first desk, and wrote – wrote, wrote…By writing at
the instant the very heartbeat of life is caught.

After you have exhausted what there is in business, politics, conviviality, and so on - have found that none of these finally satisfy, or permanently wear - what remains? Nature remains.

The dirtiest book of all is the expurgated book.

Clear and sweet is my soul, clear and sweet is all that is not my soul.

Oh captain my captain.

The untold want, by life and land ne'er granted, Now,
Voyager, sail thou forth, to seek and find.

I am to wait, I do not doubt I am to meet you again / I am to see to it that I do not lose you.

To have great poets, there must be great audiences.

Give me juicy autumnal fruit, ripe and red from the orchard.

Agonies are one of my changes of garments.

Be not dishearten'd -- Affection shall solve the problems of Freedom yet; Those who love each other shall become invincible.

A child said What is the grass? fetching it to me with full hands; How could I answer the child? I do not know what it is any more than he.

The strongest and sweetest songs yet remain to be sung.

Behold I do not give lectures or a little charity, when I give I give myself.

Why are there trees I never walk under but large and melodious thoughts descend upon me?

Unscrew the locks from the doors! Unscrew the doors themselves from their jambs!

I am for those who believe in loose delights, I share the midnight orgies of young men, I dance with the dancers and drink with the drinkers.

Oh, to be alive in such an age, when miracles are everywhere, and every inch of common air throbs a tremendous prophecy, of greater marvels yet to be.

I refuse putting from me the best that I am.

My lovers

suffocate me! Crowding my lips, and thick in the pores of my skin, Jostling me through streets and public halls...coming naked to me at night, Crying by day Ahoy from the rocks of the river...swinging and chirping over my head, Calling my name from flowerbeds or vines or tangled underbrush, Or while I swim in the bath....or drink from the pump on the corner....or the curtain is down at the opera.....or I glimpse at a woman's face in the railroad car; Lighting on every moment of my life, Bussing my body with soft and balsamic busses, Noiselessly passing handfuls out of their hearts and giving them to be mine.

I bequeath myself to the dirt to grow from the grass I love, If you want me again look for me under your bootsoles.

I am the poet of the Body and I am the poet of the Soul,
The pleasures of heaven are with me and the pains of hell are with
me, The first I graft and increase upon myself, the latter I translate
into a new tongue.

Whoever is not in his coffin and the dark grave, let him know he has enough.

Only themselves understand themselves and the like of themselves, As souls only understand souls.

To the real artist in humanity, what are called bad manners are often the most picturesque and significant of all.

Oh while I live, to be the ruler of life, not a slave, to meet life as a powerful conqueror, and nothing exterior to me will ever take command of me.

I think I will do nothing for a long time but listen, And accrue what I hear into myself...and let sound contribute toward me.

I meet new Walt Whitmans everyday. There are a dozen of them afloat. I don't know which Walt Whitman I am.

Poor boy! I never knew you, Yet I think I could not refuse this moment to die for you, if that would save you.

The sum of all known value and respect, I add up in you, whoever you are.

Henceforth I ask not good fortune. I myself am good fortune.

This is the city, and I am one of the citizens/Whatever interests the rest interests me.

"

I too am not a bit tamed, I too am untranslatable.

"

Copulation is no more foul to me than death is.

The poet judges not as a judge judges but as the sun falling around a helpless thing.

"

When I give, I give myself.

"

I henceforth tread the world, chaste, temperate, an early riser, a steady grower.

You must not know too much or be too precise or scientific about birds and trees and flowers and watercraft; a certain free-margin , or even vagueness - ignorance, credulity - helps your enjoyment of these things.

Of Equality

--as if it harm'd me, giving others the same chances and rights as myself--as if it were not indispensable to my own rights that others possess the same.

For we cannot tarry here, We must march my darlings, we must bear the brunt of danger, We, the youthful sinewy races, all the rest on us depend, Pioneers! O pioneers!

A simple separate person is not contained between his
hat and his boots.

Here the frailest leaves of me and yet my strongest lasting,

Here I shade and hide my thoughts, I myself do not expose them,
And yet they expose me more than all my other poems.

A perfect writer would make words sing, dance, kiss, do the male and female act, bear children, weep, bleed, rage, stab, steal, fire cannon, steer ships, sack cities, charge with cavalry or infantry, or do anything that man or woman or the natural powers can do.

I wear my hat as I please, indoors or out.

And as to you life, I reckon you are the leavings of many deaths, / No doubt I have died myself ten thousand times before.

Do you guess I have some intricate purpose? Well I have, for the Fourth-month showers have, and the mica on the side of a rock has.

"

A blade of grass is the journeywork of the stars.

"

I lean and loaf at my ease...observing a spear of summer grass.

I see great things in baseball.

I am larger, better than I thought; I did not know I held so much goodness.

Stand up for the Crazy and Stupid.

I pass death with the dying and birth with the new-wash'd babe, and am not contained between my hat and my boots.

There was a child went forth every day, And the first object he looked upon, that object he became...

Surrounded, detached, in measureless oceans of space.

And I or you pocketless of a dime, may purchase the pick of the earth.

I swear I will never mention love or death inside a house,
And I swear I never will translate myself at all, only to him or her
who privately stays with me in the open air.

"

And whoever walks a furlong without sympathy walks
to his own funeral drest in his shroud.

"

Freedom: to walk free and own no superior.

"

I dream in my dream all the dreams of the other dreamers,
And I become the other dreamers.

"

They do not sweat and whine about their condition, they do not lie awake in the dark and weep for their sins, they do not make me sick discussing their duty to God, not one is dissatisfied, not one is demented with the mania of owning things, not one kneels to another, nor to his kind that lived thousands of years ago.

The words of my book are nothing, the drift of it everything.

If the wind will not serve, take to the oars. To me, every hour of the light and dark is a miracle.

The United States themselves are essentially the greatest poem.

I will not descend among professors and capitalists.

You must habit yourself to the dazzle of the light and of every moment of your life.

Dazzling and tremendous how quick the sun-rise would kill me, if I could not now and always send sun-rise out of me.

The efflux of the soul is happiness, here is happiness, I think it pervades the open air, waiting at all times, Now it flows unto us, we are rightly charged.

The press of my foot to the earth springs a hundred affections, They scorn the best I can do to relate to the.

I inhale great draught of space...the east and west are mine...and the north and south are mine...I am grandeur than I thought...I did not know i held so much goodness.

Sail Forth- Steer for the deep waters only. Reckless O soul, exploring. I with thee and thou with me. For we are bound where mariner has not yet dared go. And we will risk the ship, ourselves, and all.

And as to you death, and you bitter hug of mortality . . . . it is idle to try to alarm me.

In the confusion we stay with each other, happy to be together, speaking without uttering a single word.

Silence? What can New York-noisy, roaring, rumbling, tumbling, bustling, story, turbulent New York-have to do with silence? Amid the universal clatter, the incessant din of business, the all swallowing vortex of the great money whirlpool-who has any, even distant, idea of the profound repose......of silence?

O the joy of my spirit--it is uncaged--it darts like lightning!
It is not enough to have this globe or a certain time,
I will have thousands of globes and all time.

Simplicity is the glory of expression.

Has any one supposed it lucky to be born? I hasten to inform him or her it is just as lucky to die, and I know it.

Give me solitude — give me Nature — give me again, O Nature, your primal sanities!

I will be your poet, I will be more to you than to any of the rest.

Not one escaped to tell the fall of Alamo,
The hundred & fifty are dumb yet at Alamo.

Of all sad words, of tongue or pen, the saddest are these: 'It might have been.' Let's add this thought, unto this verse: 'It might have been a great deal worse.

I exist as I am. THAT IS ENOUGH. If no other in the world be aware, I sit content. And if each and all be aware, I sit content.

Be composed--be at ease with me--I am Walt

Whitman, liberal and lusty as Nature, Not till the sun excludes you
do I exclude you, Not till the waters refuse to glisten for you and
the leaves to rustle for you, do my words refuse to glisten and rustle
for you.

The past and the present wilt. I have fill'd them, emptied them, And proceed to fill my next fold of the future.

I do not ask who you are, that is not important to me,   You can do nothing and be nothing but what I will infold you.

I find letters from God dropt in the street, and every one is sign'd by God's name...

One world is aware and by far the largest to me, and that is myself, / And whether I come to my own to-day or in ten thousand or ten / million years, / I can cheerfully take it now, or with equal cheerfulness I can wait.

The scent of these arm-pits is aroma finer than prayer....

I said: "Baseball is the hurrah game of the republic!" He was hilarious: "That's beautiful: the hurrah game! well — it's our game: that's the chief fact in connection with it: America's game: has the snap, go fling, of the American atmosphere — belongs as much to our institutions, fits into them as significantly, as our constitutions, laws: is just as important in the sum total of our historic life.

What doesn't kill you leaves scars, ruins your lungs, dries out all your tears, leaves you lying awake at 4 in the morning wishing you weren't alive.

WOMEN sit, or move to and fro — some old, some young; The young are beautiful — but the old are more beautiful than the young.

Why should I be afraid to trust myself to you? I am not afraid, I have been well brought forward by you...

I think of few heroic actions, which cannot be traced to the artistical impulse. He who does great deeds, does them from his innate sensitiveness to moral beauty.

Talk not so much, then, young artist, of the great old masters, who but painted and chisell'd. Study not only their productions. There is a still higher school for him who would kindle his fire with coal from the altar of the loftiest and purest art. It is the school of all grand actions and grand virtues, of heroism, of the death of patriots and martyrs — of all the mighty deeds written in the pages of history — deeds of daring, and enthusiasm, devotion, and fortitude.

This is what you shall do: Love the earth and sun and the animals, despise riches, give alms to every one that asks, stand up for the stupid and crazy, devote your income and labor to others, hate tyrants, argue not concerning God, have patience and indulgence toward the people, take off your hat to nothing known or unknown or to any man or number of men, go freely with powerful uneducated persons and with the young and with the mothers of families, read these leaves in the open air every season of every year of your life, re examine all you have been told at school or church or in any book, dismiss whatever insults your own soul, and your very flesh shall be a great poem and have the richest fluency not only in its words but in the silent lines of its lips and face and between the lashes of your eyes and in every motion and joint of your body.

In our sun-down perambulations, of late, through the outer parts of Brooklyn, we have observed several parties of youngsters playing "base", a certain game of ball...Let us go forth awhile, and get better air in our lungs. Let us leave our close rooms...the game of ball is glorious.

I see Hermes, unsuspected, dying, well-beloved, saying to the people, Do not weep for me. This is not my true country, I have lived banished from my true country—I now go back there, I return to the celestial sphere where every one goes in his turn.

From this hour, freedom! Going where I like, my own master...

O Mother, to think that we are to have here soon what I have seen so many times, the awful loads and trains and boatloads of poor, bloody, and pale and wounded young men again — for that is what we certainly will, and before very long. I see all the little signs, getting ready in the hospitals, etc.; it is dreadful when one thinks about it. I sometimes think over the sights I have myself seen: the arrival of the wounded after a battle, and the scenes on the field, too, and I can hardly believe my own recollections. What an awful thing war is! Mother, it seems not men but a lot of devils and butchers butchering each other.

I believe that much unseen is also here.

Walt Whitman
1819-1892

References & Further Reading
Works from Walt Whitman

Leaves of Grass (1855–1892):

"Crossing Brooklyn Ferry" (1855)
"Hush'd Be the Camps To-Day" (1865)
"I Sing the Body Electric" (1865)
"A Noiseless Patient Spider" (1891)
"O Captain! My Captain!" (1865)
"One Hour to Madness and Joy" (1860)
"One's Self I Sing" (1867)
"Out of the Cradle Endlessly Rocking" (1859)
"Patrolling Barnegat" (1856)
"Pioneers! O Pioneers!" (1865)
"Prayer of Columbus" (1900)
"Song of Myself" (1855)
"Song of the Open Road" (1856)
"This Dust Was Once the Man" (1871)
"When Lilacs Last in the Dooryard Bloom'd" (1865)

Walt Whitman

Free...

Receive a Kindle Edition in the series for FREE...

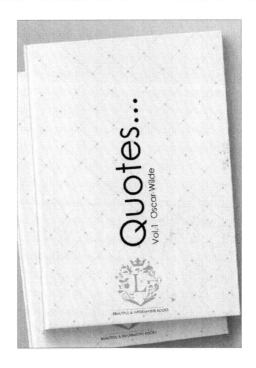

Sign up at

www.the secret libraries.com

Find us on:

The Secret Libraries

Published by The Secret Libraries
www.thesecretlibraries.com
Annotation and Artists Background by The Secret Libraries 2016

Paperback:
ISBN-13: 978-1540743459
ISBN-10: 1540743454

For more information please find us at:

www.theSeCreTlibraries.com

Thank you for your purchase.

Printed in Great Britain
by Amazon